Dedicated to Paul Whiteman

RHAPSODY IN BLUE

by

George Gershwin ™

An Explanation of the Characteristic Rhythmic Figures in the «Rhapsody in Blue.»

Throughout the "Rhapsody in Blue," George Gershwin employs a specific accent pattern that gives the music its strong rhythmic individuality,—thus:

(The same pattern, of course, may be applied to a series of 4 *eighth* notes or 4 *quarter* notes.)

The above pattern is based on the principle of re-grouping a series of 4 *sixteenths* into groups of 3 *sixteenths*. To emphasize this re-grouping, accents are placed on the 1st of the group of 3 sixteenths. This causes a *backward shifting* of the accent in successive beats,—from the 4th *sixteenth* in the first beat to the 3rd *sixteenth* in the second beat, to the 2nd *sixteenth* in the third beat, and finally back to the 1st *sixteenth* in the fourth beat. The effect is that of an exciting cross-play between two types of accentuation,—groupings in 4's and groupings in 3's.

Care must be taken not to play the accented groups of 3 *sixteenths* as *triplets*. The player should keep in mind the metrical accent, corresponding to a conductor's beat, which comes on the 1st of every 4 *sixteenths*. This serves as an anchorage for the counter-play of the accents of the groups of 3 *sixteenths*.

Gershwin has given this basic accent pattern as many as *nine* different treatments.

The *first* example is on page 3, last measure. Here is also an example of the difference between a *triplet* (on the second half of the first beat) and the accentuation on the following groups of 3's. Similar examples are on

    page 4, measures 1 and 2.
       " 7, measures 6, 7, and 8.*

A *second* treatment is found on page 6, measure 10, beginning on the second half of the first beat (ordinarily the 3rd *sixteenth* of the beat). The cycle of accents in 3's is continued according to the original chart. The left hand takes the first note of the group of 3's and the right hand takes the remaining two *sixteenths*. Note here again the contrast between the opening *triplet* and the following accented groups of 3's. It seems as though the composer wanted that distinction marked. Similar examples are found on

    page 7, measures 2, 3, 4, and 5.
       " 38, measures 11 and 12.
       " 39, measures 7, 8, 9, 10, 11, and 12.

A *third* treatment is found on page 8, second measure. The accentuation in 3's starts on the 2nd *sixteenth* of the first beat, and continues according to the original chart.

Note that the second *sixteenth* of the 3-group is divided into two *thirty-seconds*.

A *fourth* treatment is found on page 10, measures 4, 5, 6, 7, 8, and 9, and on page 11, measures 1, 2, 5, 6, 7, and 8. (Here the pattern is in *eighth* notes instead of *sixteenths*.) The right hand takes the first two notes and the left hand takes the third note of the 3-group. Note that a *triplet* ends the measure and serves again as contrast with the preceding groups of 3's. The orchestra also brings out the pattern.

A *fifth* treatment is found on page 18, measures 7, 8, 9, and 10. (Here, too, the pattern is in *eighth* notes.) The first *eighth* of the groups of 3's is divided into two *sixteenths* which rush up chromatically. The second and third *eighth* notes of one group and the start of the next group are always the same note, from which the chromatic progression ascends.

A *sixth* treatment, perhaps the most striking and difficult one, is on page 27, measures 5 to 12, in the left hand. Again the pattern is in *eighth* notes. A *quarter* note, however, takes the place of the second and third *eighth* notes. The general effect is that of a brilliant waltz accompaniment in the left hand against a syncopated fox-trot in the right hand.

A *seventh* treatment is found on page 28, measures 4 to 7, in the left hand. The pattern now has the *quarter* note as a unit, though it is divided into *eighth* notes forming stretches of tenths.

An *eighth* treatment is found on page 31, measures 5 to 8. The pattern is in *eighth* note values, the third *eighth* being a rest. The accents, however, always fall on a metrical beat,—the first and third beats of one measure, and the second and fourth beats of the next measure.

A *ninth* treatment is on page 33, beginning at the bottom of the page and continuing to the middle of page 37. The pattern, the same in each measure, is now in *sixteenth* notes. The left hand takes the first note and the right hand takes the second and third notes of the group. There are only two such groups of 3's in a measure, and the left-over two *sixteenths* are divided between the left and right hands. The accents, though, are on the first and second beats of the measure. However, on page 34, measures 5 to 8, the accents, always in the left hand, fall into the 3-group pattern of the original model.

These ingenious variations of the original pattern are enriched with sparkling melodic and harmonic devices, and abound in extremely clever keyboard manipulations,—all attesting to the creative resourcefulness that marks the genius of George Gershwin.

HENRY LEVINE

* This pattern was not unknown to the old masters. Johann Sebastian Bach used it in a *thirty-second* note figure (without accents) in his «Chromatic Fantasy» for piano:

Gershwin, however, gives such groupings of 3's a distinctive rhythmic flavor by accenting the first note of the group.

Rhapsody In Blue
for Piano and Orchestra

GEORGE GERSHWIN ᵗᵐ

Piano Solo
with 2nd piano
in score

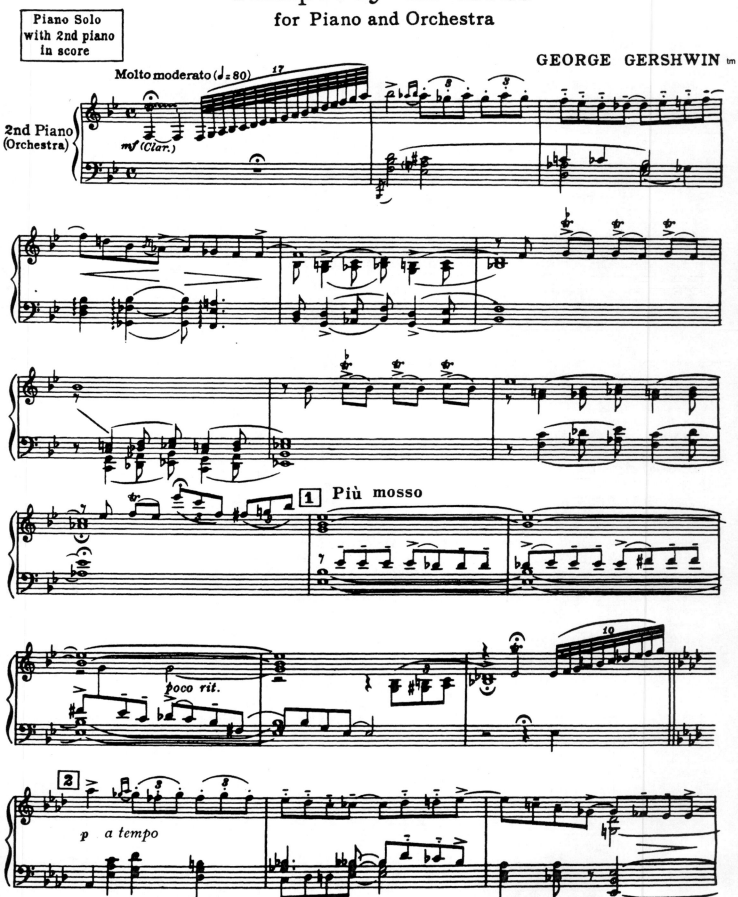

N. B. Optional Cuts: A to B, C to D, E to F, G to H.

7206-41

19 C Meno mosso e poco scherzando
(Slower and marked)

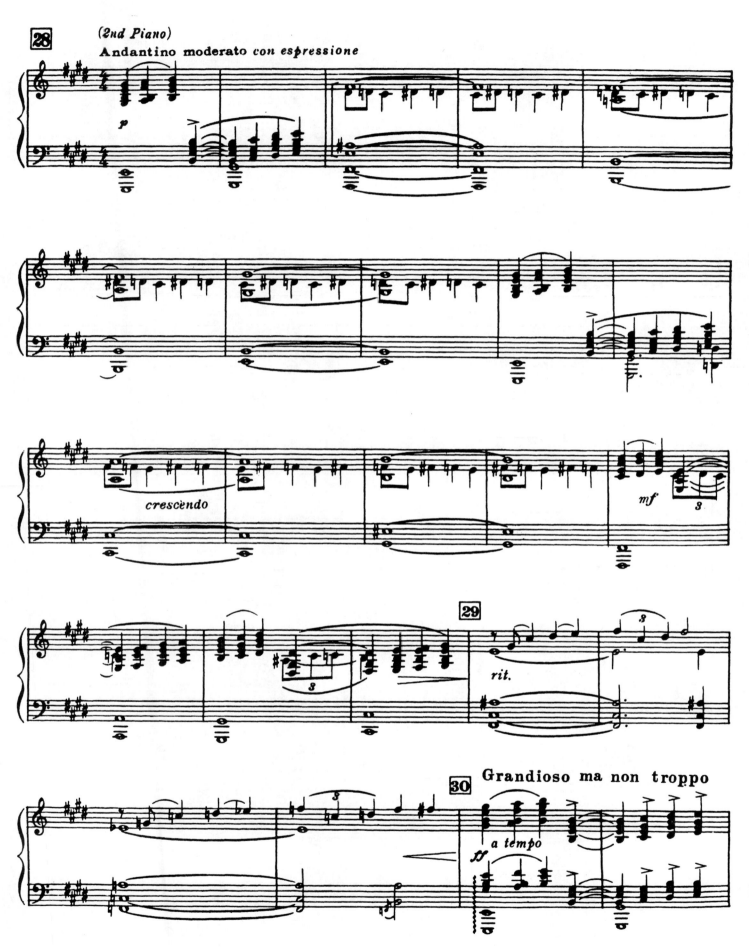

Poco rubato

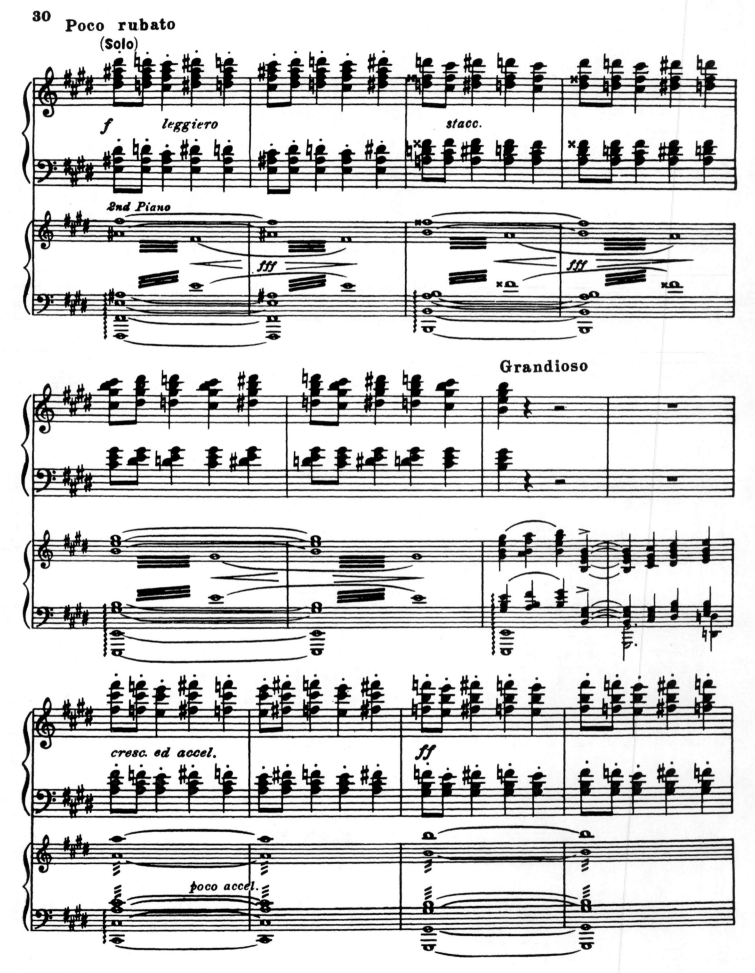

34

7206 - 41

40

Molto marcato

Grandioso (not too slow)

42

7206-41